T0065533

THE CALL TO HINDUISM IN AMERICA

Why Americans should Embrace Hinduism

JACQUES COOKSON

authorHOUSE®

AuthorHouse™
1663 Liberty Drive
Bloomington, IN 47403
www.authorhouse.com
Phone: 833-262-8899

Published by AuthorHouse 10/28/2020

ISBN: 978-1-6655-0604-5 (sc)
ISBN: 978-1-6655-0603-8 (e)

INTRODUCTION

In this book I want to talk about Hinduism and why I think it's so beautiful. In my humble opinion it's perfect in every way and I think the more people who learn about it and practice it the better off we'll be. Why do I call this book The Call to Hinduism in America and not just The Call to Hinduism, or something that doesn't sound so exclusive? Well the simple answer is I'm American, these are my people and that's who I know the best. I know the culture, the life, everything. Maybe if I tried explaining these things somewhere else it might come off wrong. So for that reason I'm aiming this at my fellow Americans. However if anyone else wants to read it I'm cool with that, I'm not mad at you and I hope you gain something good from it.

I feel like I should also say a few words about myself before I go in on this book. My name is Jacques Cookson but my friends call me xhaxhi (pronouned jaw+jee), it means uncle. I'm from a small city in southern Illinois not far from St. Louis, Mo. I come from a for the most part non practicing Catholic background. However I've always been a seeker of spiritual knowledge (I'll touch on why I think some people are like this later in the book). I've studied several different religions ranging from different Christian sects, to Islam and Paganism. I fell in love with Hinduism from reading the Bhagavad Gita. My favorite translation is The Bhagavad Gita, A walkthrough For Westerners, by Jack Hawley. I can't recommend it highly enough, please go out and get it, it's also available on Audible. I think you'll enjoy it, it will really open your eyes. Who's God? Why we're here? What happens in the afterlife? what's the point of life? The answers to complex questions that everyone has about spirituality are there.

As I mentioned, I come from a secular Catholic background. My grandmother would occasionally go to Mass, once in a while she'd go on a streak of attending mass every sunday for a couple months and then fall back into once a month or just holidays for a while. We were very close and as I lived with my grandparents I'd often go with her. I was baptized and confirmed in that church as well. She always said she felt better after mass and she was proud to be Catholic but she really didn't know much about the religion itself. If you would've asked her "Tell me something about Catholicism?" she probably wouldn't have much to say. My father and aunts and uncles went to Catholic school but none were very religious at all after leaving home.

All that being said, I was always curious. I was never really satisfied with the idea that Jesus died on the cross for our sins. Why would an all powerful God need to create a son only to have him die by human hands so that he, the God could forgive people their sins?? Couldn't he just forgive at will?? Why would he have to bargain with humans? It's very illogical and doesn't make much sense. I also couldn't accept that people could really go to a burning hell for eternity for such trivial things, including those who don't accept Jesus as the savior. This didn't seem very merciful and loving to me. I was equally frustrated with the fact that whenever you ask about any terrible event or unfortunate situation that would come up in the news and current events people would shush me with "Well it's just part of God's plan" and "God works in mysterious ways". But for a true seeker like myself, we're not satisfied with that and we search for a deeper understanding. Like a lot of people I was intrigued with the idea of reincarnation. This actually made a lot more sense to me than eternal heaven and hell but Christianity rejects this idea outright. Of course now I know that Christianity must hold onto the eternal hell dogma because it's a useful tool for scaring gullible people into believing. And scaring already believing people into staying.

As a lover of history, I was interested in Indo-European Paganism. Their temples, mythology, beliefs and practices. I wondered often what happened to these great religions? I found the answer, which I explain in this book. But make no mistake that Christianity absolutely was the killer of Paganism in Europe, The Middle East and North Africa in the classical age and the Americas in the imperial age.

My study of Paganism led me to Hinduism and the Gita. There is a connection between Indo-European Paganism and Hinduism. There are shared similarities between Hinduism and some of the Indo-European religions. Reincarnation, meditation, cremation of the dead, and similarities in some of the Gods and Goddesses. Neoplatonism, a school of thought in the pre Christian Roman world is very similar to the Hindu school of thought Advaita Vedanta. So much so that for me I think it's beyond coincidence. Could Plotinus have gotten information from some Hindu holy men? Or maybe he acquired the knowledge himself from deep meditation on the divine truth? Look into Neoplatonism and you'll see what I'm talking about.

After reading the Gita, my eyes were opened. The Gita absolutely explained everything crystal clear. It was then I decided that Hinduism really is the truth. I began reading other books, started practicing, meditating and going to temple. Fast forward years later and I feel like there's no question I can't answer when it comes to my religion. Although I'm not a karmaless renunciate living in the forest. I have a family and a job and lead a "normal" life in the material world but I am a devoted Hindu, an American Hindu who takes his religion seriously and wants to let you all know about it. To let you all know how beautiful this religion is, the rituals are wonderful and even doing puja at home on your home altar in front of your deities with candles and incense burning can be a beautiful thing. And the philosophy of the religion itself is head and shoulders above the abrahamic religions. It's like comparing college to kindergarten. As soon as I opened my eyes to Hinduism man, I was embarrassed that I ever believed any of that other stuff.

For me Hinduism answers my questions much better than any other religion and I'll also explain why I believe so later. Since finding Hinduism I feel like everything makes perfect sense, Hinduism explains everything. If someone asks me a question about why this and that is so, I can answer directly and don't have to fall back on a dogmatic statement like "Because the almighty commands it" or some fantastic story that sounds unbelievable to modern ears. I can just shoot from the hip and answer with my knowledge. If it's not obvious already I want to make it clear that I'm not an English major, I write like I speak so don't expect a lot of fancy writing but I think you'll find the content is legit. Without further adieu, let me begin.

HOW CHRISTIANITY BECAME THE DOMINANT RELIGION OF AMERICA

To explain this we have to go back in time about 2,000 years to a time when most of Europe, the Middle East and North Africa were part of the Roman Empire. At this time the entire empire was practicing a wide variety of pagan religions. There was no religious dogma the way that we see now and religious tolerance was the rule of the day. A roman soldier from say France could get stationed in Egypt and develop an affinity for the goddess Isis and upon returning to France could open a temple to Isis and everyone would be cool with it. You could have whatever Gods/Goddesses and beliefs you wanted.

When Christianity first arrived on the scene from the Middle East it was tolerated by the pagan majority who just saw it as yet another sect who happened to believe in a different way. It was after all a small Jewish sect in the beginning and Judaism was known and accepted across the empire. No one at the time could imagine that there could exist a religion that wanted to end all other religions and make itself the only one. This idea was completely alien to the people but that is exactly what happened. For reasons still unclear to us today the Emperor Constantine (The First) decided to convert to Christianity and pass laws favorable to the Christians and their clergy, giving them power and authority and ensuring that his successors would be Christian Emperors and further his anti pagan agenda.

It's not true that European paganism was dying and people converted voluntarily in mass to Christianity because it was the better option. This is latter day propaganda.

The truth is Paganism was still thriving and going strong up to Constantine's time and even for a little while after up until it was made illegal. Temples were still being built and renovated, festivals were still being held and Emperors were still praising the Gods. It was Constantine's conversion and his pro Christian, anti Pagan agenda that spelled the end of paganism. A special mention should go to the Emperor Julian, a member of Constantine's dynasty, also known as "Julian the Apostate" to his enemies. He was raised Christian but reverted back to Paganism and upon becoming Emperor began undoing Constantine's pro Christian laws and promoting Paganism again. Unfortunately, he died in the third year of his reign while on campaign in Persia. I truly believe that had he reigned as long as Constantine, he could have indeed righted the wrongs of history and returned paganism to its rightful place as the true faith of the people. Julian is an unsung hero of Paganism that is rarely mentioned. In this author's humble opinion there should definitely be a holiday in his honor, perhaps on his birthday, November 17th. If you have an audible account and are interested in the topic please listen to "The Fall of the Pagans and the Origins of Medieval Christianity", it's one of the "Great Courses" series by Dr. Kenneth Harl. He explains this situation beautifully.

The Christians who for centuries were championing the virtues of tolerance and minority rights quickly threw these ideas away and turned on the pagans once they took the reins of political power. Temples were burned or turned into churches, idols were broken and people were converted to Christianity by various methods of torture, corecsion or bribery. Those who resisted were killed. Within a few centuries Paganism was being practiced only in the European Northern and Eastern hinterlands where the church's influence was still minimal at best.

It's the descendents of these Christianized Europeans who later settled America. They continued the dirty business of spreading Christianity by force when they forced it on the native Americans and on the Africans brought over here as slaves as well. All that being said, it's easy to see why Christianty has been the dominant religion here since colonial times.

The funny thing is most Americans particularly most white Americans don't even realize that they themselves are also the victims of Christian conquest. They're the first victims of Christian conquest. In modern times they almost always have to be reminded that Christianity didn't start in Europe and was forced on them by the ruling elites of the time who had for various reasons embraced Christianty and had something to gain from it's spread. When you do remind them they often don't have a response other than maybe something like "Well ya, but that was a long time ago". They collectively have Stockholm syndrome, they've come to love and identify themselves with their oppressor. I'm hoping with education we can change this.

SPIRITUAL REVIVAL, AWAKENING

On a positive note I do think we are seeing an impressive spiritual awakening in the country. Yoga studios are popping up even in small towns. You see more and more spirituality shops opening up too that sell esoteric books, idols, incense, puja supplies, ect. I read an article a few years back that says around 25% of our population believes in reincarnation. Getting a psychic reading and burning sage to get rid of evil spirits or bad energy have become a thing. None of these things come from Christianity. In fact I imagine a good many Christian big wigs are probably getting a little worried about this because they see their dominance is being threatened.

Although some in the Hindu community aren't fans of the new age spirituality movement, I myself am a big fan. Because I think it's a step in the right direction. Lord Krishna says in the Gita that in this age we are living that is so full of bad behavior and anti spirituality that a person who merely inquires about spiritual knowledge will take rebirth in a better life than they had in this present one. I've had the absolute pleasure of visiting Salem, Massachusetts a few times. And if you go there you will see esoteric book shops, Pagan stores and various related shops and places and whatnot, particularly downtown. It's become a real Pagan Mecca here in the States and I think it's great. If you have the opportunity, go there and check it out sometime. And for Halloween they really go all out because from what I understand this is a major holiday for them. Salem is an amazing place and I tip my hat in admiration and respect.

Basically someone who comes to new age spirituality has taken a long walk down the right path and with just a little more searching and encouragement will find enlightenment.

TRIGGER WARNING

I'm not normally a hater. However this book is called The Call to Hinduism in America and not the call to something else for a reason. I want to point out why I'm choosing Hinduism and to do that I have to do a little comparative religion and I'm going to keep it real asf. So this is sure to generate some heat. If you have thin skin stop right here and maybe have a smoke before you continue.

CRITIQUE OF THE ABRAHAMIC RELIGIONS

First I'll summarize Abrahamic theology then I'll expalin further when I talk about Christianty and Islam because they changed it a little bit to suit their needs. Abrahamic theology goes back to Judaism and basically says that there's one powerful and almighty God who punishes and rewards for what he deems as good and bad. They have a list of do's and don'ts, those who God has decided are bad will be thrown into burning hell for eternity, those who are good go to a heavenly abode for eternity. Anyone who follows a different religion and worships someone besides this one God is also going to hell.

Because we're in America I'm gonna assume this theology is pretty familiar to most of my readers. So what are my problems with it? I hope you packed a lunch because this might take awhile: Just off top one of the 10 Commandments in the Bible says "Thou shall have no other Gods before me". Ok, what other Gods is he talking about if it's just him there? This to me gives us a hint that at the time this was written there were other nations, tribes, people around the Jews who had different religions and pantheons of Gods and the Hebrew God was just considered the God of the Jewish people alone. For instance there were probably the Babylonian Gods, the Egyptian Gods, the Philistine Gods and the Hebrew God. I don't think the Jews who wrote the Bible ever imagined or intended that one day their God would be worshipped by nations of non Jews worldwide. They just believed the Jewish people were a powerful people and their God, the Hebrew God was uppermost.

Hell and eternal fire for the condemned. I don't agree with the belief that someone's immortal soul can be sent to burn for eternity for mistakes made in a single lifetime. For instance if someone lives to be 86 years old and another lives to be 22, the 86 year old had an entirely full life to learn from their mistakes, accumulate wisdom and life experience. They also had plenty of time to pause and reflect on spiritual matters in later life. The 22 year old on the other hand died at the point when people are usually sowing their wild oats so to speak and committing the most sin, let's be real. In the Abrahamic tradition those two people will be judged on the same scale even though the 86 year old may have done the same things the 22 year old did at his age, he had the fortune of living 64 more years to get it right. The 86 year old will attain the heavenly abode and the 22 year old will go to hell. Is that just?? Is that mercy? I don't think so. What about people who die at 5, 9, 12 years of age? How does God judge that? Is it merciful for anyone's soul to burn for eternity regardless of their crimes?

Historical and geographical mistakes in the Bible. The famous story of Noah's Ark when two of every animal were gathered on a single boat for the duration of the flood and afterwards repopulated the earth. This is the most obvious error. This was obviously written by a guy who didn't know that certain animals exist only in certain places: A llama or a guinea pig in S. America, a kangaroo in Australia. Can you imagine the grand Odyssey of two guinea pigs walking from Peru to the Middle East crossing oceans, mountains and jungles to get on the Ark and then walking back again to Peru once the flood was over?? What a story that would be! That would really be one for the ages. Our historians today now believe the Ark story borrowed heavily from an older story known as the Epic of Gilgamesh which would have been known in the time the bible was written. The Epic of Gilgamesh itself was bogarted from an even older Akkadian story called "Atra-Hasis", and the Atra-Hasis was bogarted from the even older Sumerian Creation Myth. Some Abrahamics will respond to my guinea pig analogy by saying "Maybe this was just a local event and wasn't world wide". This makes the most logical sense but if it was a local event then why does the bible say the world flooded?? **So Xhaxhi, what do you think happened?** Well we can't dismiss the fact that the Epic Of Gilgamesh predates the biblical version and was known to the people then. Because the Epic of Gilgamesh was part of an older creation myth, and the Atra Hasis which is also somewhat of a religious text. This suggests maybe that the people of the time believed the Epic of Gilgamesh was canon and really happened. The Jews simply flipped the script a little bit, removed Gilgamesh and some other parts of the story, added their guy Noah, the Hebrew God and company and made it their own. It's also obvious that the author of the Bible really believed the animals in his area were the only animals in existence and the entire world was small enough to be within walking distance for any of them to get on the Ark in the set time Noah had to get ready for the flood. To me it's crystal clear, it's 100% bogarted from the Epic of Gilgamesh.

This is one example among many, a google search or youtude search of mistakes in the Bible will yield numerous examples like this. Strangely enough at the time the bible was written there were glorious civilizations in China, India, Crete, South America, but none of them are mentioned. Why? Wouldn't God know about these other places and want to tell his followers? Of course God knows about them. But the author of the Bible didn't! He seems to only mention Persia, Egypt and Babylonia, what does these nations have in common?

They're all in close geographic proximity to each other in the Middle East! Is this a theological problem for them? Maybe not but it proves the if nothing else the bible was written by an author from the Middle East that was completely ignorant of the world outside of his local area and not a divine being with unlimited knowledge of the Universe.

The three Abrahamic religions, Judaism, Christianity and Islam are like a somewhat normal mother and her two mean ass daughters. Of the three, the mother Judaism is the best one simply because it doesn't seek to impose itself on anyone else. To it's credit it is more tolerant than it's two daughters. With the exception of Palestine and it's direct neighbors and instances where Israel has some vested interest you rarely hear of any Jewish religious terrorism or beefing. And even when there is a beef, it's usually a reaction to something that has been done to them. They've peacefully coexisted in Europe and the Americas for centuries with little to no problems to speak of coming from their side. Even in the Ottoman Empire where Jews and Christians were second class citizens for most of the Empire's history Jews were big players in the Ottoman economic sphere and got along splendidly for the most part with their Muslim overlords. Of course we all know they have been on the receiving end of violence and oppression from both of their daughter religions many times over the years but a violent response from the Jews has been very rare. I think you'd have to go back to Roman times and some of the Jewish revolts against the Romans for such an example. While I strongly disagree with Judaism's theology, I don't see it as a necessarily bad religion or a threat to world peace and stability.

Jacques Cookson

Christianity theologically is different from Judaism because it's added ideas and scripture onto the Bible in the form of the New Testament detailing the life and times of Jesus. The Christians of course believe Jesus is the son of God sent to save humanity by dying on the cross. If you just stop right there and analyze just that alone before we even go any further you'll see it sounds strange already. Why would the all powerful God who is known to be more than a little jealous from his old testament stuff need to create a human offspring to sacrifice himself so the all powerful God can forgive humans for their sins?? It's illogical, doesn't make sense.

What do I think happened? First and foremost I don't believe for a second his mother was a virgin. If your wife came up to you and told you she was pregnant with the child of God before you even had sex with her would you believe it?? Of course not! But because this happened a long time ago, people tend to give it a pass. People, just because something happened a long time ago don't make it true. Most likely she was having an affair with another dude. Tradition tells us that she was much younger than her husband Joseph, maybe she had a boyfriend her own age before she even got married and her marriage was arranged by her family. She was from a conservative Jewish background, she could've gotten stoned to death for this so she made up some crazy story about how this is God's baby and somehow got her new husband to believe it. There were Jews at the time who were saying Jesus' biological father was a Roman soldier with the surname Pantera. There could definitely be some truth in that. I'm more likely to believe that than Mary's version, let's keep it 100. I think Jesus was a religious Jew running around Roman Palestine at the time telling people he was the messiah. <u>He was probably one of many people doing this.</u> Even in our times you'll have these guys pop up from time to time. But in our time we have science, better access to knowledge, reasoning, scepticism and logic. Most of us are not so easily fooled by smoke, mirrors and bullshit and these people are almost always eventually exposed and run out of town. However in Jesus' case he gained a small following, caught the negative attention of the Jewish big wigs, they thought he was causing problems so they had the authorities take him out. His followers were devastated, didn't want to accept that he was dead and told themselves and others he would come back, he was a savior and so on. A perfect storm of events happened that allowed this myth to catch fire, and because almost the whole western world was one big country, the usual problems of travel and language were a non issue and this small jewish cult became a sect and then a religion that would dominate the world to the detriment of classical european, african and middle eastern civilization.

The destruction of the culture of the classical world brought on by Christianity was like nothing seen before or sense. It's rivaled only by it's younger sister religion Islam. Before Christianity every city in Europe and North Africa was thick with incense smoke from offerings at the countless temples of countless Gods and Goddesses who'd been worshipped for millenia. Within just a short time Christian soldiers and mobs were destroying all said temples to the point that none remained as active places of pagan worship and only a handful remain today as ruins for tourists and archaeologists to look at or were converted to Christian churches.

Islam theologically is very close to Christianity, they believe Jesus was a prophet who could perform miracles and was born from the virgin Mary but they don't acknowledge him as the son of God. The main difference between the two religions is that Muslims have the Prophet Muhammad who came about 500+ years after Jesus and added a lot onto early church Christian theology including their main holy book, the Quran. I really believe that Islam was probably originally a heretical Christian sect that evolved into it's own religion for many reasons. Top 3 among these would probably be that Muhammad's first wife's uncle was a guy named Waraqa ibn Nawfal, he was a priest or monk in a heretical Christian sect and when Muhammad first decided that he must be a prophet, Muhammad went and spoke to him about it and asked him based on his knowledge if he thought he (Muhammad) was a really prophet or not and Waraqa said "yes". Ok, why would someone who's not a Christian seek the blessing and confirmation of a Christian priest?? The answer is they wouldn't.

Secondly, the elephant in the room is the fact that they have so much in common with Christianity. They acknowledge the Bible and the New Testament as canon as long as it doesn't conflict with the Quran and hadith (sayings of Muhammad). They acknowledge the virgin birth of Jesus and accept his miracles as legit. Ok, where did they get these ideas from?? From Christianity, obviously right?

Lastly, in Muhammad's time Christianity was still trying to find itself. Although they had come to some agreements at various councils and what not and had made a lot of progress towards Christian unification in Europe and North Africa there were still some heretical sects existing on the eastern frontier of the Byzantine Empire that were just out of reach of mainstream christian control. The Arab world and points east were just such a place. Just as an example there was a Christian sect called Docetism that believed Jesus could not possibly have been crucified, it was just made to appear so to make people think he'd been crucified. You may be surprised to hear this but this also happens to be the Islamic belief about the crucifixion. Am I saying the Docetism evolved into Islam?? Not necessarily but I am pointing out that this belief was going around out there at the time and would have been known to people in that part of the world particularly. Could it have influenced Muhammad? Or at least Muhammad's wife Khadijah's uncle? Most definitely, beyond a shadow of a doubt.

Some of the stories from the Quran talk about Jesus speaking when he was still a baby and bringing clay birds to life. These stories are also found in The Infancy Gospel of St. Thomas and The Syriac Infancy Gospel both of these books are older than The Quran. They had been declared hetertical by the the mainstream Church but were still in use by some Christians in the Middle East and points beyond at the time of Muhammad. Could these have influenced Muhammad and he decided to put them in the Quran?? I have no doubt that's exactly what happened.

These books are known as **Christian apocryphal texts**. When mainstream Christianity was still deciding "ok, what's

13

going to be canon what's not?", these books were thrown out. But as I mentioned there were still some sects on the frontier who weren't down with that agreement and kept the texts. There are other Islamic stories clearly borrowed from Christian apocrypha, a simple google or youtube search will lead you to more information. Please, please seek these out for yourself, don't just take my word for it.

The main problem with Islam though is not just the theology, it's in it's fanatical zeal to spread itself around the globe by all means necessary. It's hardcoded into the Quran and hadith that Islam is to be spread even by sword point, jihad. Abu Bakr Al Baghdadi, the founder of ISIS once said, "Islam has never been a religion of peace. It's a religion of fighting". Jews and Christians are given a choice between between paying protection money jizya, converting to Islam, leaving the country (even tho it may have been theres to being with) or death. All others; Pagans, Hindus, atheists, ect are just given the options of convert, leave or die. The choice of paying protection money (jizya) is not an option for them.

<u>Do all Muslims believe in this jihad doctrine?? What about my Muslim neighbors, they seem cool. They're good right??</u> All practicing Muslims that adhere strictly to the Quran and Sunnah do believe it. Because they don't believe the Quran was simply "divinely inspired" like Chrsitians and Jews believe in regards to the Bible. The Muslims believe the Quran is the word of Allah (God) directly. So one mistake renders the whole book and religion null in their eyes because Allah doesn't make mistakes, right? Therefore when the Quran calls people to jihad, if they're being honest they

can't deny it, because denying it would be denying the Quran is legit, feel me? Do you think ISIS, Al Qaida, The Taliban, ect, ect.. are pulling their beliefs out of the blue?? No of course not, it's a fundamental part of the religion and in their eyes they're just being proper Muslims and doing God's will honestly. They would actually say that the Muslims calling for religious harmony and peace are the heretical ones. And according to Islamic scripture they would be right.

Are there really kind and peaceful Muslims? Absolutely, but these people are kind and peaceful by nature. They would be kind and peaceful no matter what their religion or lack of religion is. A lot of these folks are in fact Muslims by name and culture but not necessarily strictly practicing the religion itself. They've decided to put tolerance and humanity above religious dogma, at least in public anyway.

FINAL THOUGHTS ON THE ABRAHAMICS

I personally think all the Abrahamics have this tendency for spreading themselves violently in their DNA. It comes from ancient Judaism, you'll see it in the Old Testament where God commands the Jews to kill everyone in Palestine and make it their homeland. However the Jews never tried what the Muslims did because although the Jews wanted to conquer a homeland strictly for themselves they were never interested in converting anyone to Judaism and spreading the religion itself. Once they had Palestine in hand, they declared it the Kingdom of Israel and stopped there. I think the Jews probably consider their religion somewhat as an ethno-religion. I'm not sure they would even want to try to convert the world to Judaism even if they could.

Christianity has a very long history of trying to spread itself through violent means. In fact it's only been in the last couple centuries that it stopped trying to spread itself through violent means. Secular and humanistic thought beginning in the renaissance era has slowly overtaken religious fanaticism in the western world. To give Christianity some credit, the teachings of Jesus were peaceful and tolerant anyway. I don't think there's anywhere in the New Testament where Jesus commands his followers to make war on his enemies or kill them. It took additions from kings and church leaders later to shape Christianity into the violent religion it became for so long.

Theres an arguemnt that since Judaism and Christianity overcame their fanaticism over time that maybe Islam because it's related will soon follow suit. Although this argument has some logic to it, the problem is that a Christian or Jew in our times can dismiss violent verses in the Bible as archaic and things that aren't done anymore. But a Muslim can't dismiss violent verses in the Quran as some archaic practice because they're hamstrung by that consept that the Quran is God's word dirctely and is a message for all times. If they deny it then it takes them out of the fold of Islam basically. The only way that argument could become true is if bigwigs in the Muslim community came out and said bascially, look the Quran is not directly from Allah but it is divenely inspired. That would give the Muslim community at large the breathing room necessary to disimiss those verses. **Will that happen tho??** I highly doubt it because whatever bigwigs had the bravado to suggest this would be so loudly shouted down by the orthodoxy. I can't imagine any of their scholars being so brave, even though I think there's many of them who believe it in their hearts. Very unfortunately, I think they'll probably take their doubts to the grave rather than subject themselves to such career ending ridicule and criticism. A lot of these guys probably have years invested in study, they probably make their living as professional Islamic scholars. If they came out and said "I've arrived at the conclusion this is all false."? They would have their integrity, but their name would be mud in the eyes of their community and they'd be jobless. Some of them probably continue this charade just for keeping their financial security, this goes for Christian scholars as well. I've heard Mother Teresa in her old age was questioning her faith but kept going because she'd had a lifetime invested in being a nun and didn't know what else to do.

ON PAGANISM

Notice I didn't title this chapter A critique of Paganism, consider this rather as a hug of Paganism more than anything. I actually love Paganism, I embrace it and you Pagans are my brothers and sisters. I think the neo pagan movement is a glorious thing. I'm with you all the way, I hope we can rebuild what was lost in the old times. However... I need to say this and please take it with a big glass of love and respect.

I don't think the religions we had before the Christian Age can be completely reconstructed as they were. At best what can be created is a mix of what we do know about those religions and whatever people come up with now. Rather that be mixing it with Hinduism, Buddhism or other religions to try to fill in the gaps or maybe a council of Pagan bigwigs of various paths sitting down somewhere like in Salem Massachusetts (That would be kinda cool. Call it The Council of Salem 2025 or whatever) and have a council to try to hammer out some form of canon, a name to rally behind, organize a clergy, make an agreement for temples and shrines, ect like the Christians did in the early church. Until there's a moment like that I think Paganism is always going to remain a bunch of solitary practitioners doing things their own way and never having direct contact with each other. There may be a handful of small groups in bigger cities that get together occasionally but that's probably the best it's going to get.

So what is the problem with that? Nothing as long as you're content with that. But for a lot of people having a sense of community, communal gathering and worship and a support system is of the utmost importance and should never be underestimated. I would actually go so far as to say a lot of people probably leave Paganism and go back to their previous religion just for this reason. Barring a grand council and a mass pagan organizing, what can be done about this? I just so happen to have the answer and this is why I wrote this book my friend and I'll get to that later.

ABOUT HINDU THEOLOGY

This is going to be difficult for some of my readers to wrap their head around. Especially those who have only been exposed to Abrahamic teaching. The thing is, there is no one all encompassing theology for Hinduism. Hinduism is like an umbrella term for many different paths that come out of India. I personally follow the Vaishnava school of thought. We worship Lord Vishnu as the supreme deity and adore his many incarnations like Krishna and Ram and Ram's devoted friend Hanuman and the Goddess Lakshmi. But some Hindus believe Lord Shiva is supreme, some believe the Goddesses are supreme, some believe all the Gods are equal and don't have any particular favorites. But even with all those differences, all are still considered Hindus, worship at the same temples and accept each other's opinions without issue. However, I would say that all Hindu schools of thought have 3 concepts in common; Karma, Samsara and Moksha. For lack of a better term and also borrowing a term from Islam you could say these are like the three pillars of Hinduism. Let me explain:

Karma- You hear this word a lot but most people don't realize this word comes from Hinduism and is a Hindu concept. Karma is not the name of a Goddess who punishes the bad and rewards the good. It's just a natural law of action and reaction. Just fix it in your mind that the word "Karma" basically means "action".

If you put your hand on a hot oven it's going to get burned. If you jump off a building you're eventually going to hit the ground, and depending on how high the building will determine how bad your fall will be. If you cause suffering you yourself will eventually suffer, if you cause happiness you'll receive happiness. Every living thing is subject to the law of karma and the karma of every living thing is connected to the karma of everyone else. Like threads in a rug. My actions will affect other people and depending on how big my actions are, it will affect a few or a lot of other people. This is karma in a nutshell but I'll continue to expound on it throughout the book because it's a major concept in Hinduism.

Samsara- This is the cycle of birth and rebirth. In Hinduism the material body is made of biological material and subject to disease and all manner of death but the soul is eternal and can never be killed and never dies. It just returns eventually in a new material body based on your karma from the previous life/lives. There is no Heaven and Hell exactly in Hinduism. There is a spiritual world and many places within that spiritual world and then there is also the material universe where we are now. When someone dies they don't have to reincarnate immediately, if they have a lot of good karma built up they can stay in the spiritual world for a long time before they have to come back.

In Hinduism we believe the universe goes through repeating cycles called Yugas that last thousands of years. Some yugas are better than others. At present we are in Kali Yuga, the worst yuga when unrighteous action is common and righteous action is rare. Although the yuga is not good and we're gonna be in Kali Yuga for many more millenia it does have one advantage, Lord Krishna says in the Gita that in this age one who merely inquires about spiritual knowledge will have a better rebirth and merely chanting the names and mantras of the Gods is great karma in your favor and will lead to a good rebirth. An ideal rebirth would be to take rebirth as a celestial being, a demigod in some better material world than this one. This boon is granted because righteous action is so rare and it's so easy to just go with the flow of adharmic (unrighteous, anti religious) behavior that even the slightest good karma is worthy of a great boon.

Moksha- Moksha is the concept of permanent liberation from samsara. Your soul is composed of your jiva and your atma. This is in fact the real you. The atma is a little spark of the paramatma, the supreme soul, the God of the Gods, the formless energy responsible for all creation including the Gods/Godesses. Your atma separated from the paramatma at the creation of the universe. When you achieve moksha you return back to the paramatma and don't need to return to the material world ever again, even when the universe is destroyed and created again you will remain in bliss with the paramatma.

How is this achieved? By having no karma. **How do you have no karma??** By having no attachment. Someone who has no attachment to anything can never be affected by karma. Lord Krishna says that to such a person a lump of dirt will have the same value as a nugget of gold. They want nothing and expect nothing, they are the same in moments of honor and dishonor. Typically people seriously trying to achieve moksha will go off on their own to live in the mountains or forest or maybe a monastery wearing only simple clothes and living off the food and charity of others or off the land itself. This is to distance themselves from possible attachments. These people are called Sanyasis, Sadhus or renunciates they never eat for pleasure, rather only to give themselves sustenance because one can become easily attached to the taste of food. They spend all their time meditating, praying and doing spiritual practice. Some of them travel, walking from city to city. In India there is a huge festival called the Kumbh Mela that attracts Sadhus from all over and it is the largest pilgrimage/festival in the world. Hindus from all over the world go there.

Is it hard to achieve moksha? Yes, it's almost impossible. In fact achieving moksha is a bit like hacking the system of samsara. Because your natural state is to be in samsara, to escape from samsara and return to Godhead is a bit of a rebellion from the natural order. To put it in simple terms you have been here since the creation of the universe and you're still here. That should tell you how hard it is. In fact, I would argue that we should be realistic, if we have to ask if Moksha is hard to achieve then we are probably not going to achieve it in this lifetime. Don't worry about moksha, focus on a better rebirth, if you keep getting a better rebirth with every incarnation then maybe at some point you will take rebirth in a situation where detaching from material pleasure and seeking moksha realistically may be more of a possibility.

I may be alone in thinking this but I believe it's entirely possible that some people could have achieved moksha but instead chose to come back again as a celestial being, a demigod and then acquired some karma and got stuck again in samsara.

Eventually everyone will achieve moksha. This is because at the end of the universe, everything returns back to Godhead. Back to the singularity that it started out as. At this point you can say everyone has achieved something like temporary moksha. However, Lord Brahma will create it again and the cycle will begin again. This happens infinite times and never stops. At this point you'll return again to the material universe.

The Gods and Goddesses: Remember what I said earlier about "Hinduism" actually being an umbrella term for a lot of different somewhat related paths. Now you're going to see how that comes into play. In fact the real name of the religion is "sanatana dharma", it means something like "The eternal way" but for the sake of ease of conversation most people refer to it as Hinduism or Hindu dharma. And myself I'm going to call it "Hinduism" in this book just to keep it simple. My opinion of the Hindu pantheon is not going to match everyone's else's opinion. However, again like I said before in Hinduism it's perfectly normal to have different opinions in these matters. Welcome to Hindu dialectics.

There are 3 major Gods in Hinduism: Brahma, Vishnu and Shiva. Each of these Gods has a female Goddess counterpart, they are Saraswati, Lakshmi and Parvati respectively.

Above these Gods in the pantheon is the Paramatma. The Paramatma is the Godhead, the shapeless, nameless energy that created even the Gods, it's the source of all things. Below Brahma, Vishnu and Shiva are countless Gods, Goddesses, demigods and various celestial beings. Even the 3 major Gods and Goddess can take various different forms with different names. Parvati for example can take the form of the famous Goddess Kali. Lord Vishnu has 9 different avatars that have come to earth so far. A 10th avatar, Kalki will come at the end of Kali Yuga. Each of the 3 major Gods has a role in the universe. Brahma is the creator, Vishnu is the sustainer and Shiva is the destroyer. As we know, the universe is cyclic, so when Shiva destroys it Brahma will make another one. In fact this isn't the only universe, Lord Brahma is constantly creating universes, this is his dharma so to speak.

I'm having a great internal debate whether to give my opinion on the rank of the Gods, who is "supreme" who is a "demigod", ect. I've decided not to do that because I don't want to have that much influence in your spiritual practice. I'm afraid there may be a lot of people reading this who are completely new to Hinduism and will take everything I say as canon. Maybe this might even be their first book on Hinduism and they'll think "Well, Xhaxhi said we should worship x, y, and z. So it must be so.".

I think it would actually be more Hindu of me to let you decide for yourself. I'll just merely give you the tools and you can decide how you're going to use them. For those genuinely interested in Hinduism, please, please, please... don't stop studying at this book. Keep going, read the

Bhagavad Gita and the Ramayana. Read and watch the work of trusted gurus, use the internet, there is so much information out there that you'll grow old and die before you stop learning.

<u>Maya</u>: Maya is the veil of illusion that shrouds the material world. It's what make you believe that your material body is the real you and not just the shell carrying your soul. It's what makes people bedazzled by attachment and blind to dharma. Unseen to the naked eye, everything in the material world is dripping with maya. I'm sure some people will be like, **Xhaxhi, I'm still not sure exactly what you mean. Can you give us a good example of maya?** It's like this my friend, imagine if you will, someone who buys fancy clothes because they like the attention and compliments it gets them from other people. To this person it will seem like such a great thing to get this attention and whatnot and it'll make them feel like they are really something special. But when you peel away the maya and examine this situation unveiled you can see that the compliments they're getting are just coming from the egos and attachments of other material bodies who desire them. Those material bodies in turn are just feeding the attachment to attention of the person wearing the clothes and none of this is of absolutely any real positive value. In fact this can lead to a multitude of bad karma (anger, desire, jealousy, etc..). But this person can't see any of this because they are completely blinded by maya and only notice the material world. Money, material objects that people become attached to, even houses and cars are all just maya because they are of the material world. These things seem to have importance and value but it's

only because we've attached value to them. **But Xhaxhi, houses, cars and money are necessary to basic survival! No one can live without them! How can you say they are maya??** They're "necessary" to survival if you're attached to maya. Like most of us including myself but they're not really necessary to survival. A yogi living in a monastery or in the mountains, someone who's serious about achieving moksha wouldn't find these things necessary, because he's not attached to maya. But for those of us living in the matrix, so to speak, ya those things are pretty necessary. **Do you really have to give up these things to achieve moksha?** Yes, because to achieve moksha you can't have karma. To have attachments is like opening the door and letting in the wind and the wind is like karma. It's almost promised if you have attachments you're going to have karma. But like I said earlier, don't worry about moksha. Just focus on making good and limiting bad karma. You have forever to get moksha.

<u>Idol worship in Hinduism:</u> Some people particularly those of an Abrahamic background have a hard time dealing with this subject because it's so frowned upon in the all 3 Abrahamic religions. But I think it's actually one of the most beautiful parts of Hinduism. There is just something about the incense, the candles and the idols that really pleases me. Probably from past memories and attachments.

The Abrahamics, particularly Muslims have an absolute disdain for idols. And their biggest criticism is always something like "That idol is just made out of stone, how can it be God? It can't do anything. It makes God angry, ect". I'll address their first criticism first, that's it's only material and can't be God. This is true, we know that it's only material, however there is a great story about this from Indian history. A king once summoned a swami to court and said to him something like "Swamiji, how can you worship these idols? They're nothing but wood and stone and they can't do anything". The Swami pointed to a painting of the King on the wall behind him and told the guard "Take down that picture of the King and spit on it." The king was really shook and angry and the guard was too scared to even try it. The swami said to the guard "What's wrong? It's just paint and paper, it's not really the King. Go ahead, spit on it." When the guard refused, the swami spoke again, "You see, the picture is not the King exactly but in a way it is. It has the essence of the King, when you look at it you automatically think of him." The King then spoke up and thanked the swami for for insight and told him he changed his mind about idols.

The idols, usually called murtis and deities in Hinduism are like that exactly. By sitting in prayer in front of an idol of Lord Krishna for example. Looking at the idol helps you to think about the Lord and focus your worship on him. When you lay from fruit on an offering plate in front of the Lord it makes you feel a little like you're offering it to the Lord himself. For me there is something special and ceremonial about idols. I think it's a wonderful part of the religion. Every Hindu home should have a puja altar with some idols on it. And every day you should light a candle, some incense and leave some fruit or beverage, food that you can eat later in the day. Once it's been offered to the Gods for an hour it becomes prasad, holy food.

ANSWERS TO COMMON QUESTIONS ABOUT HINDUISM

Here are some common questions people ask me about Hinduism. I think it's maybe better to explain things this way than trying to cover everything and possibly leaving out something simple that people might really be curious about.

Can a non Indian person be a Hindu? Of course. You will hear sometimes on the internet somewhere or just rumors that you have to be Indian to be a Hindu. This is not true. **Why do you say that?? What is the proof??** Very simple, did the Gods create the Universe or just India? The Universe of course. Also we believe in reincarnation. Someone could be born as an Indian in one life and a Missourian in the next life. The material body is not the real you, you are the atma and the jiva. A true practicing Hindu knows this.

If someone has been a Hindu for 20 lifetimes but was born in the US as a non hindu this time, can someone tell this person he or she can't be Hindu because they're not Indian in this lifetime?? Of course not. If someone sees an Indian guy sitting in church would they say, "Hey, only a white person can be a Christian."? Not anyone with any good sense. But occasionally you'll have some people who are ignorant of the true teachings of their faith and they'll say stupid things. Don't listen to these people, they're either racist or just ignorant.

Do you have to be a vegetarian to be Hindu? No, the reason a lot of Hindus are vegetarian is because it's considered bad karma to kill an animal to eat it. And I agree, even though

I am a meat eater myself. But there's no Hindu version of the Pope who's going to declare you're not a Hindu if you eat meat. Some Hindus do eat meat, just as some Muslims eat pork. There's evidence to suggest that Hindus in Vedic times weren't adverse to eating meat but I'll let you go into that on your own because that is a very controversial topic and I don't want to tackle it in this book.

We are born with the pluses and minuses of our ancestors. We were born into a culture where meat is a staple in our diet. Especially here in the Midwest where I'm from. Burgers, fried chicken and BBQ are absolutely part of life. It is what it is, most of us will probably always eat meat, it's who we are as a people. However if you want to avoid the bad karma of consuming meat, vegetarianism is strongly encouraged. It's probably better for your physical health as well. But at the end of the day like everything else in Hinduism it's up to you. The traditions and the shastras are the tools and it's up to you to use them how you see fit.

Which God should I worship? This is a very Abrahamic question. My answer is, why pick only one? You can pray to Shiva for serenity, Saraswati for knowledge and Hanuman for strength and bravery if you want to. And this is just one example. It's not as if they are jealous. Jealousy is an egoistic human attribute, it's a form of attachment, Gods and Goddesses don't have that attachment. A lot of people have an "ishta deva", a favorite God or Goddess but it's not a must.

How do I worship all these Gods? Again with an Abrahamic question, which is perfectly normal. The simple answer is you don't have to. That would be a lot of work. If you go down the cereal aisle at the store do you ever wonder, "How am I going to eat all this cereal?" No, of course not, you pick what you like and take it. You can even get one brand this week and another brand the next week. Polytheism is the same way.

Why is it that good people always die so young and bad people seem to live forever? Some of this is karmic but most of it is just a combination of nature and coincidence. Material bodies are made of biological material and biological material isn't perfect and isn't made to last forever. It deteriorates over time, can cause problems to itself such as cancer and autoimmune diseases, it is susceptible to other life forms like fungi, bacteria, other people, animals, and viruses. All these things can damage or kill a material body but the atma is immortal and will surely take rebirth in a new material body with the karma you left off with. This is hard for people of an Abrahamic background to understand but the Gods don't micromanage the material world. Sickness and death is part of nature that even they don't interfere with. If it seems that some real good dude died young and some eveil old man lived to be 100 it's not because the Gods prefer evil people, it's just because for whatever reason, aciident or sickness or murder or whatever his material body died. It's that simple.

There are also situations where a death is karmic, someone for karmic reasons had to die at a certain time of a particular whatever. But it's impossible to know if a death was karmic or not. We can only speculate. In fact some of our wisest yogis and swamis will say it's not polite to say "So and so died because of karma for ..." because we don't know for sure and it's possible to make a little bad karma by making a false statement because it can lead to false rumors and wild speculation spreading around.

Doesn't Hinduism believe in the caste system and isn't the caste system racist, classist and a bunch of other bad stuff? The late great Hindu scholar Swami Chinmayananda did an interview one time for an Australian TV show and it's available on YouTube. I'll link it at the end of the book. He explains it so perfectly that even a complete novice will have no trouble understanding it. Because I like it so much I'm going to use his explanation.

Caste system is a relatively modern bastardization of the varna system of Hinduism. The varna system is a scientific classification of psychological types. There is no escaping it, it exists whether we like it or not, in every country, with every people regardless of religion or culture. Usually after a few conversations, sometimes even just one conversation you can see their varna. There are four varnas:

The Brahmins: The intellectual and learned class, the clergical class also falls into this group. Professors, artists, philosophers, priests are good examples. In a healthy society they are the brain trust and moral compass of that society.

The Kshatriyas: The bold men of action, power players, military officers. Those who want and yield power. In a healthy society they carry out the directions of the brahmins and defend the society.

The Vaishyas: The merchant class, the money chasers, the folks who dream 24/7 about how to make money. Captains of industry, JP Morgan, Andrew Carnegie, and dudes like that are examples of successful Vaishyas. In a healthy society they keep the wheels of the economy turning without letting greed make them take too much of the money so the shudras can afford to live.

The Shudras: The working class, the people living paycheck to paycheck. The backbone of the society in many ways. The final cogs in the machine. In a healthy society they carry out the real work to keep the society going.

As you now see these types truly exist in every society. When most people say "caste" they really mean varna. And varna is not a negative thing, it's very real. But "casteism", discrimination based on caste is the real problem. **Does casteism exist?** Yes, and also in every country and with every people, it's not a Hindu thing, it's a class thing and it's not a good thing but I'm not going to try to come up with the solution in this book. But remember we need all 4 varnas working in symmetry for the society to function properly. This segways nicely into my next commonly asked question.

Why are some people rich and some people poor? That's an easy one, karma and varna. Most likely a combination of the two. The Gita tells us that however you left the world, how you were in as a person in your last life you will return back in the wombs of like minded people.

Let's say in your last life you were the type who was content just getting by, or maybe even not working at all. Not doing anything to make money. Then of course you will be born into a family that is the same way. The universe itself is cyclic: creation, expansion, and retraction (destruction). And everything is a microcosm of the universe. In this type of case, poverty is also cyclic. The majority of people born into poverty are this type in my humble opinion.

It's also possible that it's karmic retribution for a past life of hoarding money, stinginess, embezzling, greed etc. As I mentioned with karma, if you jump off a building you're going to hit the ground, either in this life or the next. You have to burn off that bad karma regardless and that's really what binds us to samsara also. This is the minority of people born into poverty in my opinion.

Varna also plays a huge part in this because whatever varna you are, you will naturally possess those skills and if you do something that requires those skills you'll do it better than someone who's not of that varna. This is what's called **dharma**, if you're a vaishya you're dharma (think duty) is the monetary pursuits. You'll just be naturally more inclined toward business and money than other varnas and if you decide to go into business you'll be more successful than other varnas would be. If you're a shudra, you're not going to have that drive towards business and money. It's not that a shudra doesn't think about money because surely they do. They may be thinking like, "Damn I wish I had the money for this or that" but then they'll turn around and do the same things they always do without changing anything. If you're a shudra you're dharma is manual labor and your mind is going to be on living life, having fun, family and working to get by and not "OMG, I gotta do whatever it takes to make this money and be successful". **What happens when a vaishya dies?** As we remember from the Gita we take rebirth in the wombs of like minded people. So now you see that often, better yet more than often, almost always wealth and poverty are cyclic. Again the universe is cyclic and everything is a microcosm of the universe. Someone born into poverty in this life was most like born into poverty in their last life, and the one before, and the one before, and the one before,.. The same with someone born into wealth.

Why do so many people pray for world peace or a cure for disease but their prayers are never answered? I hear these questions a lot. These kinds of questions come from the people who believe there's a God who micromanages everything and if only enough people pray he'll come and answer their prayers.

Let's tackle disease first. Every last one of us must marry a bride of death one day. The material body is not immortal, it's made of biological material. Biological material isn't perfect. It's capable on its own of making genetic mistakes. Cancer for example is just out of control cell replication, created by your own body because of either random or environmental factors. In fact most cases of cancer are random, one of the victim's cells missed a mistake and copied a defective cell that's now replicating itself nonstop. This proves the body's imperfection. We're also susceptible to a multitude of other diseases, viruses, infections, micro organisms, and the list goes on.

To the question at hand, does prayer help? Lord Krishna says in the Gita that Nothing that happens in this world has to do with him, <u>it has to do with nature</u> and nature itself is just one of his creations. This means that he is not the cause of the disease, it's not as if he has struck you with this disease. You have it because of nature. As far as prayers helping, it must be possible because lord Krishna tells us that praying to the Gods for material boons such as wealth, health, ect can be granted through prayer and devotion. The more difficult the situation the more devotion is required for them to do this but it's not promised. Furthermore, Swami Paramahansa Yogananda claimed in "Autobiography of a Yogi" that his guru Sri Yukteswar told him that an enlightened master could cure himself and others of any disease because he has total control of mind and body but most ordinary people arent on that level. In "Autobiography of a Yogi" there are many examples of Sri Yukteswar's healing powers. Everytime he interceded to cure someone of some disease they were cured without exception just by Sri Yukteswar's meditation and advice. It's still always best to trust in god but don't forget to tie up your horse. By all means pray and meditate but keep taking your medicine too, either ayurvedic medicine, modern medicine or both.

Nobody likes to hear this, including myself but I want to be real with you. The material body will die one day, period! Sometimes this happens to people even at a young age, sometimes to people we love and almost always it will seem unfair. This sucks, but we need to remember that the material body is finite but the soul is immortal and will surely return unless they have achieved moksha. The loved one you have lost can one day come back to you as a child, grandchild, ect. If you desire this, meditate on it and pray for it, put their picture on your puja altar if you want. They can hear you in the realm of the ancestors in the spirit world and they will make a greater effort to come back in your life when an opportunity arises.

<u>Now we'll deal with world peace</u>. Let's say for example I wake up really hungry in the morning and pray for God to take me to the donut shop so I can buy a donut, I can pray till the cows come home and he won't magically take me there, right? I actually have to walk over there or get in my car and drive. I have to perform an action, right? World peace is the same way, everyone's karma is intertwined, even if 1 million people are praying for world peace none of it matters if the Brahmins of the society have become corrupted and are coming up with reasons for war, the kshatriyas gladly make this war a reality, the vaishyas greedily make a king's ransom churning out weapons of war and the shudras happy go long with it as foot soldiers, factory workers and patriotic cheerleaders.

For world peace to happen, EVERYONE has to want it and work for it. An action has to be performed just like me driving to a donut shop. It won't just magically happen without putting in the action/karma to do it. If the whole world was dedicated to making good karma then we'd have world peace, not only world peace but an end to hunger, homelessness, the healthcare crisis and everything. Unfortunately we're in Kali Yuga and adharma (anti-dharmic) behavior is dominant in this age. Its not in the interest of those in power to have world peace. Why?? Because they're attached to money and power. Which brings me to....

What is the cause of suffering? Let me introduce you to the grandmother of all problems. Her name is Attachment. Jack Hawley's translation of the Gita (A Walkthrough For Westerners) covers this beautifully. Again I highly recommend it because it will answer pretty much all your questions about everything. I'll try my best to explain it here.

From attachment comes all problems, the two daughters of attachment are anger and desire. Anger is unfulfilled attachment and desire is attachment on steroids. From desire comes greed, theft, jealousy and infidelity. From anger comes war, violence, depression and murder. In society if the vaishyas become greedy they won't pay the shudras a living wage for their work, if the shudras don't have the money to have a desent life then anger and her offspring, depression, crime, murder and war will live among them and the society as a whole will suffer greatly for it and someone will stand up and ask the question, "**What is the cause of suffering?**" As I always say, the universe is cyclic and everything is a microcosm of the universe.

If you're not smoking what I'm rollin in regards to attachment being the root of all problems. Prove me wrong, think about any problem you have and I promise you'll find attachment at the head of it. Attachment is not necessarily always bad. You can be attached to something good. Someone can be attached to their children, they can be attached to going to the temple, they can be attached to having a roof over their head. All these are reasonable and normal. <u>HOWEVER</u>... they are still attachment and attachments no matter how good intentioned they are can lead to negative things. **What makes something "negative"?** As noted guru Sri Sri Ravi Shankar would say, "If it promises pleasure but causes pain it's negative". Smoking cigarettes for example makes you feel good for awhile but undeniably causes health problems, drinking alcohol, drugs, overeating (attachment to food) have you ever ate a really good burrito and afterwards been like "Ok, that burrito was so amazing I never need another one ever again. I'm fulfilled". No, of course you would never say that because you're attached to it and sooner or later you'll want another and another and this leads to a multitude of health problems as well.

I was talking to my youngest daughter who was 6 years old at the time and just so you know she is my absolute life. She is Goddess incarnate in my eyes and I would do anything for her. She was telling me about this little boy she's friends with and how this little boy would play rough with her sometimes and she didn't like it. I got so mad I told her to tell him if he does it again that I will come to his house and beat up his father to teach him a lesson. Was this a good thing to say? Absolutely not. Was it negative? Yes. It goes to show that even a good intentioned attachment has it's sharp edges. We just have to be mindful of it. Everyone, unless you're a sadhu living in a monastery or a sanyasi living alone in the forest is going to have attachments. Just try to remember karma at all times and try your best to promote the positive and avoid the negative as much as possible.

How to not get angry, sad and stay calm and stress free?
There's a famous story about a king named Chandra in ancient India. This dude was like the uppermost king in India in his time. He decided to call a council of all the bigwig religious dudes in his kingdom. Every sadhu, sanyasi, renunciate, priest and holy man of every stripe showed up to the palace. The King sat them down and said, "I want a mantra that's appealing to every God in every situation. One I can say in times of honor and dishonor, victory and total victory (because he'd never admit to anyone that defeat was even a possibility)." They eventually came up with a mantra but they rolled it up and put a seal on it, and told the king to open it only when he was in dire straits.

One day came when Chandra's army was defeated and Chandra himself was fleeing for his life on horseback while the enemy were close behind him. He came to a cliff and there between the cliff and his enemies he hid in some bushes. It was then that he got out the mantra and broke the seal. The mantra said real simply, "this too shall pass". At first he was mad, "This is the mantra??!" He was thinking. But with deeper reflection he realized it was true. He remembered the words of the Gita that say as sure as good times come and go, bad times will always come and go. Nothing in the material world is permanent. Long story short, Chandra escaped, rebuilt his Army and took back his kingdom. At the victory parade after he retook his capital city, he heard some people in the crowd say "King Chandra is God". He started to puff up with pride and arrogance but then again remembered the wise words of the mantra, "This to shall pass" and regained his humility.

There's an Islamic scholar named Ibn Taymiyya who lived in Syria in the 12-1300's. He said one time "What can my enemies do to me? If they kick me out of the country, this is just an excuse to travel. If they put me in prison, this is nothing more than a spiritual retreat. If they kill me, I go directly to heaven". Even though Ibn Taymiyya was a Muslim in this situation he is on point. You need to remember that at the end of the day every single one of your problems exists because you are attached to something. There's no exception to this rule bro. You can analyze any problem you're mad or stressed about and at the head of it you'll find attachment. Cut that attachment and the problem will go away. If you can't cut the attachment, then just realize that the problem is really just the attachment and then you'll have more clarity of thought on how to deal with the problem. rationally.

Remember too that you are the atma not the material body. Far too often people identify themselves with the material body and forget about the atma, their true self, completely. There has never been a time when you didn't exist and there will never be a time when you don't exist. There is literally nothing that can really happen to you ever. Everything in this world is maya bro, and the only things that can happen to you are superficial and illusionary. They bother you because you let them bother you. Just let that shit go because in reality none of it really affects anything of importance. **But Xhaxhi, how do we deal with a loved one dying, how can that not bother you??** It will bother you because that attachment is so strong. I've been in that situation myself and even I was shook. My advice on that is just as best as you can just try to remember that they're only leaving their body, they, the real them hasn't died. And they can come back in your life again as some other person in the future. And remember to pray and meditate on it, especially meditate as much as you can because by meditating, you listen to the Gods and messages from the spiritual world. Another question I see a lot is, **How do I cope with the infidelity of a spouse or partner?**

Ok, people have died for this one, people have killed for this and killed themselves and people have thrown their lives away for this issue. Let me go in on this for ya. Ok, first of all let's step back and analyze. Why did it make you upset? Probably because you feel betrayed. Why do you feel betrayed? Most likely because you loved this person and you were attached to their love, their body, their attention and you feel like they gave it to someone else. Ok, I'll stop right there. You see the root of this problem was the attachment to that person. To be attached to your children, your parents, grandparents, close family is one thing but to be that much attached to an unrelated adult in this Kali Yuga is asking for trouble. Remember that most people in this time have an adharmic (negative, unrighteous, evil) outlook on life. We're at a time when if someone says they'll do something for you, it's the same as saying "maybe". And if someone says "I swear", it's the same as saying "I'll try". **Xhaxhi, are you telling me not to get into a relationship?!** Nah, not at all. But you do need to bear this in mind at all times and not be surprised if this or something akin to it happens. Man a good rule of thumb is just don't love somebody so much that you can't live without them. And remember always the words of Ibn

Taymiyya again, "What can my enemies do to me?" Were you really affected for real by what happened?? You're still the divine atma right in a material body, you're still on the dharmic path to enlightenment right? Ok, so why you mad, some adharmi had sex with another adharmi that you let yourself get attached to. <u>Let it go</u>. Holding onto it will only leave the door open to bad karma. Sever the attachment if you so wish and move on. If you think that sounds difficult, it's really not. It sounds difficult for someone living in the darkness of maya and concerned only with the pleasures of the material world. But for someone truly thinking with a dharmic mindset it makes perfect sense.

Even after I said all that I'm 100% sure some people will be like. **"I see what you mean but I met this guy/girl, we have so much in common, ect. We won't have any problems. Do you think it'll be alright to start a relationship?** Ok, do you think if I go over there and snatch up that wild squirrel by the tail it'll be alright? Maybe if I'm really fast and don't mind getting bit, right. Because best believe you're going to get bit a few times. Why is it so difficult? Do you remember who the Grandmother of all problems is? Her name is attachment. When you enter into these relationships you're inviting her into your house. Will she be nice? Maybe sometimes, not all attachment is necessarily bad, right? But at the end of the day she is the grandmother of all problems, that's her MO, eventually she's going to serve you up some of those home fries, period. In the case of a relationship, you have two people bringing their attachments into the equation. So double the odds. Even when you look at these couples that have been together for decades and whatnot.

The secret to their longevity is usually that one or both have broken their attachments to something for the sake of preserving the relationship. I've heard a lot of people say "I don't really like so and so but I stay for my kids sake". Ok, well this person has very obviously severed an attachment to achieve a greater goal. They made a sacrifice, I would argue that was actually a dharmic move and worthy of some praise. There are a million other such scenarios of couples doing things like this. A lot of times, they'll call this "compromise". But it's really sacrificing an attachment. Look, I'm pro family for sure. I want people to have kids and I want those kids to have both parents at home and for their home life to be happy. So I'm not calling everyone to retreat into the forest and become a sanyasi, that's only for the real serious believers who want moksha. But for the rest of you just keep my advice in the back of your mind at all times. Think hard before you start a relationship, make sure both of you all are on the same page, prepare to give up some attachments and I know you're gonna hate this but don't get so attached to that person you can't live without them.

Why are some people gay, transexual, ect? First of all just let me mention that in the Abrahamic faiths they have a very difficult time with this one because they don't believe in the transmigration of souls (reincarnation). They believe you get one life and everything is God's plan, and because they think God hates gay people it puts them in a very difficult position. Because why would God make someone gay if he hates gays, ect?? It really blows a lot of holes in their dogma and really puts a stoplight on the falsehood of their religion.

Point blank, it is what it is. I get a good laugh watching them try to field this question.

Now, onto the reason. Ok, the simple answer is reincarnation. The more complex answer is that your atma is not alone when it travels to a new body. Your atma is pure soul, the spark of the divine but your atma is shrouded in a kind of subtle body called the jiva that contains also your ego, your ego contains your past life memories, personality, varna, karma, attachments, likes and dislikes, ect.

As for transexual people: Let's say someone had been a woman for the last 20 lifetimes and they very much enjoyed being a woman and they developed an attachment to womanhood, femininity, and all that entails. And then later after a death for some karmic reason they had to take rebirth as a man, their soul (meaning the whole atma, jiva package) can still be attached to being a woman and they'll still feel like they're as feminine as any woman even though biologically they're a man. This is normal and people shouldn't be angry with these people or persecute them. Angry for what? Past life attachments of other people? Who doesn't have them? In fact, the existence of trans people shows our Hindu Dharma is correct and reincarnation is real. Jai shri Ram (Praise Lord Rama).

Does race and or ethnicity play a part in reincarnation?
Yes and no. Let me explain. Although a soul can take rebirth in any human form, the fact is that most people if karmically possible will take rebirth in the same family because of the ego's attachment to surviving family members, hometown, friends, ect. Also for reasons of familiarity it's my belief that

people will also try to come back in the same race or culture or geographic area if their karma allows.

So you see, the connection between race and reincarnation is one of attachment. It has nothing to do with if you were white last time so you must be white the next time for example.

If reincarnation is true, why don't I remember their past lives? Do you remember being a baby? Maybe just a wisp of a memory here and there. The faint memory of a lullaby or being swaddled in a loved ones arms but no clear memories. As well you may have a faint past life memory of a strangely familiar name or place or you may have an unexplained fascination with something you have no known connection to.

The truth is you still have all your past life memories, they're in your jiva (the subtle body shrouding your atma), the problem is accessing them. Think of it like your body is a computer and your past life memories are files that are stored in some hard to reach area of your hard drive. When you take rebirth, the soul (jiva and atma) enters and connects to a new material body. The jiva has memories but the new brain doesn't, the connection between the two is somewhat weak so the past life memories are just stored in the jiva. Remember that the jiva is of the spiritual nature and the brain is of the material nature. It's difficult for the material brain to access spiritual information from the jivatma. Sometimes very young kids, let's say toddlers maybe, occasionally have some past life memories that come to their mind. They may talk about an event or place that they maybe shouldn't know about. This is because they are so young and memories stored in the jiva are more fresh than they are in older people but as time goes on, memories created in your new body add up and bury your past life memories even more. As well, you'll have a lot of times someone come up in a family that has completely different likes and dislikes from everyone else in the family. Your likes and dislikes really come with your jiva. You've had the same tastes for lifetimes. You won't remember why but they're there.

To access those memories is possible but would require you to do a lot of deep meditating on it often and probably over a long period of time. It might take years but it's possible to develop your meditation skills to the point where you can access any information in your soul but most people don't have that kind of dedication and patience to learn about their past lives. Their interest in them is usually just a fleeting curiosity, so they don't have the desire to put in that much work to learn about them. But in fact most of our gurus say that it's not wise to focus on this anyway and for us to leave the past in the past. The reason "past life regression therapy" is sometimes successful in helping people recall past life memories is because it uses hypnosis and hypnosis itself is basically just a very deep guided meditation.

Is it possible to take rebirth as an animal or lower life form?
Yes, for sure. This is mentioned in the Gita as being possible. I think it's rare though, most humans will probably stay humans with just a lower or higher life based on their karma. The good news is that I'm pretty sure anyone reading this book will not take rebirth as an animal since Lord krishna says that anyone who merely inquires about spiritual knowledge in Kali Yuga

(our present age) will take a better rebirth and by reading this book it means you're inquiring. Lord Krishna also stresses the importance of what you think of in the last moments of life before you leave your body as having a major impact on your rebirth. And he says in those difficult and scary moments if you can stary focused on him you will go to him.

Usually someone who takes rebirth as an animal is someone who has a lot of negative karma, someone who kills animals for fun, someone who behaves like an animal, ect. Or one who has a lot of rajasic or tamasic tendencies. Let me explain.

What are the three gunas? They are the three aspects of your personality. All three exist in everyone. They are:

1). <u>Satva</u>: All things good, wholesome. Doing spiritual practice, making good karma, being good to others, eating healthy, going to temple, hospitality, meditatting, keeping good manners even in trying times, ect. Are all satvik activities
2). <u>Rajas</u>: Aggression, nervousness, anger, the need to be constantly doing something, seeing yourself as better than others, over working, ect. Are examples of Rajasic activities.
3). <u>Tamas</u>: Sloth, laziness, those who seek the pleasure of not doing anything are engaged in tamasic activities.

They exist in everyone but at certain times for example tamas might prevail in your life. Other times rajas, but the goal should be to try live satvik and let satva prevail most of the time in the battle between the three gunas.

Between rajas and tamas it's easier to move into satva from a rajasic position than from a tamasic position. Because when rajas prevails you have motivation to do something, the key is just to focus that motivation on satvik activities instead of working, partying, ect.

Imagine someone going to the temple to pray. A satvik person will go with simple clothes, will pray and meditate with full attention on their deities. A rajasic person will go in their fanciest clothes and pray in an exaggerated manner to show and get attention so other people will think "Wow, that guy is really serious". But in reality half the reason he came to the temple was for the attention, so people can think how great he is. A tamasic person might go just for a minute and leave early without actually doing much but more likely they'll just make an excuse not to go and stay home and do nothing beneficial. These three examples summarize the three gunas. Remember you have all these aspects operating simultaneously but try to make satva your superior guna. There is a multitude of easy to access information out there that go much more in depth on the gunas if you're curious and want to learn more.

Of the three tamas is probably the worst because at least with rajas you can become satvik with just a change of focus. With tamas to become satvik you have to change your lifestyle basically, it's a big difference but it can be done. Don't lose heart, you don't have to become a saint in this lifetime. Just try to be the best you can be and a little better each lifetime. I want to take a second to reassure some people who may be reading this and thinking "OMG I'm tamasic.

I'm going to take rebirth as an animal!" and start panicking. Ok, I'm addressing you directly now. Take a deep breath and relax. The fact that you're reading this book is satvik because it shows you care about your spirituality. Someone who cares about their spirituality won't take rebirth as an animal, especially in Kali Yuga. Should you try to change your tamasic tendencies? Of course. But again, baby steps if you must. Think of the most tamasic thing you do and try to make it satvik. Even one small thing is progress. If you manage that then try maybe another small thing and make it satvik. Samsara is a marathon not a sprint. Don't overburden yourself or burn yourself out trying to change everything too fast. If you do, you're likely to get stressed and quit.

What is Advaita Vedanta and what are your thoughts on it? Advaita is Hindu school of thought preached by the famous guru Adi Shankaracharya that basically claims non duality, God is in all things from the lowest to highest, all things are God and the only thing that exists is God and by this logic all religions are the same and equal. Since all that exists is God, then all worship of God must be correct. Advaita has a lot in common with Buddhism and some people think Adi Shankaracharya was heavily influenced by Buddhism, which is probably true. The famous youtuber Koi Fresco practices Advaita I think. A lot of people who find Hinduism from the new age path or from Buddhism end up practicing Advaita or some Advaita..ish brand of Hinduism. So what do I think about their claim that all religions are the same and equal and it doesn't matter which one you practice?

Ultimately I think it's right, Lord Krishna tells us that he comes to people however they imagine him, whatever form they imagine him he approaches them in that way. He also says all prayers come to him regardless of who is being prayed to and even when people worship demigods they are indirectly worshipping him because he is master of the demigods and he accepts all this worship and never rejects any of it. Wow, that's great right? Advaita must be the true path, right?? Well, kind of.

Here's the problem, even though fundamentally it's right, the truth is that no other religion would agree with it. If you tell the other faiths particularly the abrahamic ones that all religions are the truth and the differences are just superficial they'll all think you're crazy. And they have a point because even though all prayers go to the same address, the other religions have added so much dogma onto their religious practice that it renders advaita's one religion theory useless. A muslim for example will say you have to testify that there's no God but Allah and Muhammad is his messenger, as well as all of their other dogma. Christians will say you have to accept Jesus as your lord and savior or you go to hell. Can advaita say these creeds are the same as advaita and have any credibility? **No. But why??**

Because the other religions aren't on Advaita's level. Advaita is looking at the biggest picture, the origin, the source of all things and saying "the goal of all religions is understanding, worshipping and being in unity with the Godhead". But the other religions aren't looking that far my friend, they're worshipping the superficial, the dogma and tradition as much as more so than the Godhead itself. They can't even wrap their heads around what Advaita is claiming because they're not looking that deep. They can't see the forest for the trees so to speak. <u>And as long as this is the case then all religions aren't the same because the other ones aren't focused on the source, they're focused on obeying dogma and following tradition, period!</u>

That being said, if you practice advaita I still love you. You're still my hindu brothers and sisters but we gotta agree to disagree. Fundamentally advaita is right, the problem is it's alone in being right. The other religions won't agree. You see what I'm saying? In every family you're going to have disagreements even among your closest family members.

Thoughts on Iskcon (The International Society of Krishna Consciousness aka Hari Krishnas) They are a Vaishnava sect that focuses primarily on Lord Krishna, the 8th avatar of Lord Vishnu. I have a favorable view of them, they do some great things. First and foremost is their outreach, they've done so much to spread Hinduism here in the US. Their temples are open to all, questions are welcomed no matter what they are and they have a free food program. Their guru Srila Prabhupada arrived in the US in 1966 and spent the last years of his life until his death preaching Vaishnava hinduism and building a significant movement. **Ok, so what's the controversy?**

The controversy is that they focus too much on Lord Krishna and consider the other Gods/Goddesses of the Hindu pantheon (Brahma, Shiva, Parvati, Ganesha) to be simply demigods. Some also feel that even Rama and

Vishnu himself are not given proper respect even though Lord Krishna is an avatar of Lord Vishnu. This leaves a lot of people feeling alienated, particularly followers of Lord Shiva and Hindus that follow the Shakti school of thought, the adoration of the Goddesses. The critics of Iskcon claim that they have basically created another monotheistic, somewhat dogmatic religion based but based on Hinduism rather than the Abrahamics. This makes some in the Hindu community consider that Iskcon isn't part of Hinduism. I however do think they're Hindu firstly because they believe in the 3 pillars; moksha, samsara and karma. Secondly they worship Lord Krishna who is a Hindu god, they revere the Gita which is a Hindu scripture and lastly they identify as a Hindu organization, sometimes they'll avoid the term "Hindu" and say "Sanatana dharma" but the two terms are the same in modern use, it's just that "sanatana dharma" is the proper term and "Hinduism" is a foreign term used for "sanatana dharma". I consider myself Vaishnava but I recognize the other Gods and Goddesses as completely valid and I have a shivling and a murti of Ganesha and Durga on my puja altar and they are shaivite deities. I would also have no problems at all going to an Iskcon temple. In fact, I think maybe if you're new to Hinduism and you're of the Vaishnava side of Hinduism maybe you should go to an Iskcon temple first because they are always actively spreading Hinduism they are more used to dealing with new Hindus and their questions. With all these in mind, Iskcon are Hindus in my eyes. Hinduism is a broad religion with room for many different opinions and ways of doing things. I like Iskcon but as with practitioners of Advaita we have to agree to disagree on some issues.

Thoughts on Swami Paramahansa Yogananda's belief that Jesus was an enlightened yogi. I'll give a little background information here for some of those who might not know. There was a Hindu guru named Paramahansa Yogananda who came here to America in the early 1900's and lived until his death in 1952. You can think of him as kind of an early version of Srila Prabhupad. He comes from the Kriya Yoga tradition. He wrote several books including his most famous one, "Autobiography of a Yogi", which is a good book by the way. He believed Jesus stayed in India for decades and returned to his homeland to preach the dharma to people in Palestine

To be honest I disagree with Swamiji on this one. **Why?** Well because don't you think a guru preaching dharma should actually be preaching dharma?? Just from what you've learned of hinduism in this book so far do you think Jesus was preaching Hindu dharma? Was he preaching the 3 pillars; karma, moksha and samsara? No, absolutely not. He was preaching the standard Abrahamic stuff except with himself as the messiah.

If someone tries to say, "Well when he said, do unto others… he's talking about karma". I find that argument really weak. If that's his explanation of karma, it is a very elementary explanation and definitely not one you'd expect to hear from someone who's supposed to be an enlightened master. Some of Yogananda's followers will also try to say that Jesus' disciples changed his message to make it something else. This argument is also laughable. Why would his disciples who were supposed to be his loyal devotees and his biggest believers change their master's message to something so counter to hindu dharma but in line abrahamic thinking? The answer is they didn't, they were just carrying on Jesus' real message. He was a Jew who fancied himself as the messiah and had nothing to do with hindu dharma, period. **So why would Swami Yogananda make such a claim?** Because he was trying to use the age old tactic of religious syncretism to appeal to the Christian masses here. Rather than ignoring or denouncing Jesus, he thought maybe if he incorporated him into the dharma he would attract more interest and have less critics. He probably felt it might also make Hinduism more relatable to the general public which at that time was definitely true. You have to remember that this was in the first half of the 1900's. America was a much more Christian nation at the time. If you were trying to bring a religious message here back then you had to at the very least give some kind of nod to Christianity.

Let me add a disclaimer and say I love swami Yogananda, he said a lot of great things and has done a lot of good. But in this particular case I very respectfully disagree but I understand why he did it.

Why are some people seekers of spiritual knowledge and so many people aren't? If you're a seeker. This speaks volumes about you. It means you're on the right track. If you're a seeker it means most likely you've always been this way through many lifetimes. If you're in this category consider yourself blessed, this is a very positive thing. The problem is oftentimes when people are seeking it's a bit like trying to find some fabled city that you've only heard about and never seen and you really don't even know which direction it's in. Some may find different religions thinking they've found the city only to realize later that they found the wrong city and return to seeking. Rajiv Malhotra, the renowned author and hindu activist has talked about his "U-turn" theory about how people will convert to a new religion, start out very devoted but will eventually for a multitude of possible reasons, become disenchanted with it, even attacking it and go back to their original religion albeit maybe with some changes. I agree with him, I've seen it happen personally. He says the way to prevent this is to engage these people and bring them into the Hindu community. Let them feel a sense of community and hindu identity, temple attendance and they will most likely not make the U-turn. This is a big reason why I wrote this book. I hope it stands as a beacon, guiding seekers to Hindu Dharma.

Do you need to have a guru to be a Hindu? No. You don't have to have one. In this country I think we have a lot of problems trusting a guru because so many con men have popped up over the years claiming to be spiritual leaders. And that mistrust can at times be a good thing.

You don't have to have a guru if you don't want to but if you can find one that appeals to you and that you trust go ahead. In my opinion It's good to have a spiritual master that you can look to for guidance and advice and direction. You don't have to know your guru personally. You can follow any guru out there if you want, there's a multitude of them; Sri Sri Ravi Shankar, Sadhguru, Swami Mukundananda, ect. Just do your research. People always say you don't have to actually go looking for a guru, the guru will find you. I personally don't have a guru, I've thought about it. Maybe if I find the right one. But I feel like if you're a legit guru, you should be living a very humble existence and teaching people for free. I think my other problem is that I have that natural American scepticism of religious leaders.

You know how it is here although it's almost always Christians here that do this, every once in a while somebody will pop up and claim they are some religious master, prophet, ect and then they'll go and do something really shady or live super large from the money their followers give them. And their followers will be like so and so is God or the right hand of God. I always get a good laugh because sometimes their followers won't even say God, they'll say Gawd, just to put that extra sauce on it to try to get their point across and let you know they're serious and you should believe in this dude. They'll be like "Jacques Cookson is Gawd!" These people really make it hard for legit gurus and religious leaders that actually have good intentions.

Is meditation an important part of Hinduism? I would actually say it might be the most important part. People have described it as "prayer is talking to God but meditation is listening to God". I would agree with that. Listen, you need to always remember that you are not your material body, you are the atma inside the body. The atma is a spark of the divine and all information, everything ever known is inside your atma. **So why don't I know these things??** Because you're trying to access spiritual knowledge with a material brain. To access this information requires meditation. Opening your third eye through deep meditation will allow you to look inward into the atma and from there the possibilities are endless. Meditation is a cornerstone of Hinduism. Peace, relaxation, spiritual knowledge beyond anything, physical and mental healing are all possible with meditation. **When is the best time to meditate?** Preferably when you have time alone in a quiet place with no distractions. But someone who's truly mastered meditation can meditate anywhere and in any situation. They can even carry on a conversation while meditating, this is called "split consciousness" when someone is able to maintain a meditative state while keeping enough attention in the material world to have a conversation, do their job, ect. Have you ever been driving somewhere and look up to realize that you'd traveled much further than you thought? Or have you been at work, working along only to realize that it's almost lunch time and it feels like you just got there? That is a type of meditative state, you were so focused on something that your consciousness slipped into meditation and you didn't even realize it. If you can harness this skill you will be a natural at meditation. The deepest meditation is before you go to sleep, laying down and meditating yourself to sleep. Meditating this way over a long period of time you can surely achieve whatever you're focusing on, be it opening your third eye of whatever. **What can meditation do??** Man what can't meditation do?! With a lot of practice, and opening your third eye, the window to the atma and accessing the knowledge of the atma you can do anything within the limits of having a material body. Seeing the future, seeing the past, communicating with people far away through your thoughts. Swami Yogananda said his guru was able to appear to his devotees in other cities from his monastery and could manifest himself in two places at once and cure disease. **How is that possible, to gain such powers from meditation? It sounds crazy.** It does sound crazy but if we set back and analyze it. What is the atma? Pure divinity, a spark of God and your true self. What can a spark of God do?? Everything right? So to make it clear, to access the atma is to access God and meditation is the way to do it. But remember, you're probably not going to meditate once or twice and open your third eye. It will probably take years of doing it all the time. If it was that easy, everyone would be able to do it. To master meditation is a magnificent achievement, but master mediation and your attachments and you're a saint. If you're a saint, you're next incarnation is looking pretty good and even your chances of moksha are on the table.

"Cultural Appropriation"?? I've seen a few posts in some online Hindu facebook groups I'm in where some people are saying things like. "I'm afraid to go to the temple because I'm worried about cultural appropriation". First of all, I don't believe in cultural appropriation. That's some bullshit made up by over sensitive people looking for something to whine about. Are you triggered if you see an Asian guy walking around in a cowboy hat? Or some foreigners using American street slang? Hell nah, I don't think anyone is triggered by that. In fact it seems like the whole world is always biting off our culture and it may be funny sometimes but there's nothing wrong with that. Cultures have been overlapping and influencing each other since the beginning of culture. This is nothing new and it's normal. Language, writing, religions, architectural styles, agricultural practices, all these things have developed as they have because of cross cultural influence. Is that "cultural appropriation"? If some people from culture A like something about Culture B, they're gonna adopt it for themselves, this is a given.

There is such a thing as mocking and insulting. But that is something else all together. But if someone admires and sees truth in something from another culture and decides to pick it up and embrace it, that's a positive thing.

WHY HINDUISM?

◇◇◇◇◇◇◇◇◇◇◇◇◇◇◇◇◇◇◇◇◇◇◇◇◇◇◇◇◇

I want to say something to those who might be afraid of leaving their current religion because they're afraid of upsetting cultural norms and upsetting religious family members. If you are of European stock, the descendent of African slaves, or a Native American. You must remember that Christianity and Islam were most likely forced on your ancestors at some point in history. Even if your familt has grown attached to Christianity or Islam and feels it's part of your cultural identity, it's really not. These people are victims of Stockholm Syndrome, meaning over time they have come to love, sympathize with and identify with their oppressors. Christianity has been in existence for 2,000 years, Islam for 1,400 years. In the great scheme of things that's not a really long time. The Pantheon in Rome is about 1,900 years old and was for a few centuries a pagan temple and is now a Catholic Church. This goes to show that there are even buildings still in use that were here before Christianity and Islam were well established. There are monoliths in Northwest Europe, pyramids of Egypt, ect that were here many millenia before Christianity and Islam. Idols have been found in Russia and Germany that are 35,000 years old or older, some are even made of mammoth bone. Those were possibly worshipped by some of your ancestors. There were classical civilizations in Greece, Italy, Crete, Egypt, Mesopotamia, India, China, Latin America that were doing spiritual practice and were doing just fine without Christianity and Islam. Were these folks not your ancestors?? Don't let anyone lead you to believe the world will come to an end if you leave your current religion. Remember that at some point in your family history someone left their old religion and took up the one you have now. You won't be the first person in your family to change religions, that's a promise. You might be the first in living memory but so what? That's not a big deal.

I know that in Islam, the the punishment for leaving is death. But here in the US my friend, they can't legally enforce that. They might be like a little Chihuahua and do a lot of barking and bouncing around but probably won't actually bite or they'll face the hammer of our justice system and they know this. In this country you're free to choose any religion you want, or no religion if you want. This is enshrined in our constitution and no one can take it away from you.

Hinduism explains things the Abrahamics cannot: The Abrahamics believe in an afterlife that consists of heaven and hell. If someone obeys God's command they go to heaven, if not it's hell. And people go to hell for the smallest of things committed in a single lifetime and their soul burns for eternity. They like to claim their God is merciful but where is the mercy in this?

In Hinduism we don't have Heaven and Hell, there is the material world and the spirit world, both worlds have various good and bad places. When you take rebirth you start off with the karma you lest the world with last time. So if you lived to be 86 or you lived to be 22, your next life you just pick up where you left off karma wise. Some people have the misconception that when a person dies they return immediately to a new body. This is not the case, you can stay 1,000 years or more (or less even) in the next world before taking another rebirth if your karma allows it.

The Abrahamics have no answer to why there is suffering or happiness for that matter. They will claim it's all part of God's plan but if that's the case then God's plan must be completely random because why is this particular individual suffering and why was this person born into such a good situation? But in Hinduism this is easy answered by karma and makes much more sense. There is no God's plan to it, it's all part of natural law just as much as a seed leaving a dying plant and taking rebirth again in the soil somewhere else.

The Abrahamics don't say much about the soul. They seem to think a new soul is created every time a man and a woman make a baby. But in Hinduism we know that souls have been in existence since the creation of the universe and just migrate from one material body to the next.

Community and place of worship: This is particularly aimed at my pagan and spiritual readers because they don't really have that place of communal gathering and place of worship generally. But Hinduism has it, anytime the temple is open you can go. If you're shy about going, go when there's not many people and maybe talk to the priest then and explain your situation. Or call the temple or message them on social media, most temples are on facebook these days. Iskcon (The international society of Krishna Consciousness) a vaishnava Hindu sect with a storied history here in the States has a lot of American devotees and any of their temples would definitely welcome you and your questions if you're so inclined. If not, the other temples will welcome you as well. No one is going to be mean to you or kick you out, you can't build a temple in America and forbid Americans from going there. It'll be ok, they might be curious and ask a bunch of questions but they'll be happy to see you.

Some people are not familiar with all the Hindu holidays, they don't know when they are, what their significance is and don't know how to celebrate them. If you don't celebrate the Hindu holidays that's fine. We've all grown up with Christmas, Easter, Halloween, Thanksgiving, ect. They're ingrained in the culture and even though a lot of them have Christian connotations they're celebrated even by secular Americans as a day of getting together with family and enjoying a good day of feasting and fun. By all means you can continue to celebrate them and whatever other holidays you celebrate. Maybe in the future if you want you can start to celebrate the Hindu holidays as well. But I completely understand that when you grow up with certain holidays your whole life, adding new ones just doesn't have the same magic. Take baby steps in this matter. In the big picture these holidays are merely side commentary.

In every scenario where you can compare Hinduism to any other religion or philosophy, Hinduism in my eyes wins hands down. Even stepping back and looking at it from outside I can't see anything else as being better. Even if you read this book just for the information and not seeking to become Hindu necessarily that is fine. I hope you gained at least a better understanding. For the seekers of spiritual knowledge who read this book I hope you learned something as well and were able to get what I'm trying to say.

IN SUMMARY

◇◇◇◇◇◇◇◇◇◇◇◇◇◇◇◇◇◇◇◇

I believe we're in the beginning of a big spiritual awakening here and you're going to see more and more of us embracing Hinduism and in the future you'll see a lot of Americans going to the temple like they do the church. I sincerely hope it'll be a normal thing that nobody will think twice about.

I think this religion is perfect for us for a couple reasons. For it's tolerance and its individuality. Two important things that are highly valued here in this country. In hinduism there is no dogmatic one set of rules or one certain way to worship. You have complete freedom in this matter. There are a multitude of deities and you can worship whatever ones you see fit. When it comes to doing puja at home, by all means personalize it however you want. You can get inspiration from the temple or friends, or online for that matter but at the end of the day it's your altar, your deities and your puja. Not to mention you'll be able to burn sage and incense, go to psychics, practice yoga and use herbal medicine all judgement free without having to justify it to your abrahamic friends and relatives. There is a complete science in hinduism on herbal medicine, it's called ayurvedic medicine.

If you're pagan and already worship Thor, Odin, Cernunnos, Zues, ect. by all means you're free to put them on your altar and incorporate them into your puja. If you're in this case, nothing really changes for you other than you're gaining a place of community worship, the temple and you're gaining the shastras (the scriptures) of Hinduism that will fill in the gaps for you that paganism doesn't have.

It was a pleasure writing this book and I hope you enjoyed it, Your brother, Jacques Cookson.

SOURCES/RECOMMENDED READING

*"The Fall of the Pagans and the origin of Medieval Christianity" The Great Courses lecture series by Dr. Kenneth Harl.

"Caste you cannot remove it. Understand what caste is?" Swami Chinmayananda on caste on youtube

*"The Bhagavad Gita, A walkthrough for Westerners" by Jack Hawley

*"The Ramayana" by Krishna Dharma

"U-turn theory" by Rajiv Malhotra

"Autobiography of a Yogi" Paramahansa Yogananda

ABOUT THE AUTHOR

Jacques Cookson is a native son of Quincy, Illinois but currently lives and works in Eastern Iowa with his wife and youngest daughter. He is a graduate of Western Illinois University in Macomb and holds a bachelors in biology. He is also an avid student of history with particular interest in ancient and medieval Europe and the Near East.

Mr. Cookson, is an unapologetic Hindu and strong advocate for spreading Hindu dharma. He believes Hinduism is facing a crisis similar to that faced by European Paganism at the end of the classical age. The Abrahamic faiths are investing a lot of energy into converting Hindus to Christianity and Islam particularly in India and Hindus must fight fire with fire and actively spread their religion as well to the four corners of the globe. At the same time he believes America is going through a spiritual rebirth and awakening and could benefit greatly from Hinduism.